# "All Wrong"

## Self-Evaluation

## Things we do WRONG in relationships

Unless indicated, all scripture quotations are taken from the Holy Bible: Living Version.

Scriptures quotations marked KJV are taken from the Holy Bible: King
James Version.

Grateful acknowledgements are hereby expressed to those who have
granted permission to include copyrighted materials in this book. Any
inadvertent omission of credit will be gladly corrected in future editions.

This book is dedicated to Pastor E.V. Hill SR. my family and friends and
the Mt. Zion Missionary Baptist Church for all the support.

Special thanks to Antonia Porter, Leija Ford, Kedron Carey, Angie Dillard,
Tanisha Baisley, LaMonica Beasley, Netta Trice, Stormie Lampkin,
Shamika Mc Elroy, Kimberly Hicks, Tasha Porter, Stephanie Arwine and
my entire family for pushing me to complete the book.

FIRST EDITION

Jacket Designed by Willis T. Brown

Jacket Photograph by Willis T. Brown

Editorial Services by: Tinna Marie

ISBN- 978-0-615-43157-4

# *"All Wrong"*

# ℬ Contents ℘

# ℬ PURPOSE ℘

The purpose of this book is to stimulate your mind, challenge what you see, think, and know about relationships. This is **not** a book that will give you all the answers to why men and women do what they do in relationships. Nothing in this book is new or something you may have never heard or read before, but it is the way we will approach it, and present it to you.

We hope it will open your eyes to the slight mishaps and misfortunes we all make while in relationships.

I am not trying to be all philosophical, and I am definitely not a **therapist** by any stretch of the imagination. Although: I should have looked into that field when I was in college. But because we are human, and **God has given mankind the unique ability to choose**, we are subject to making many errors when we are lead by our own **emotions,** and **ideas**.

My hope is after reading this book you will evaluate yourself, significant others, friends, associates, and acquaintances, who you find yourself in a relationship with.

## Let's start with some of my favorite quotes:

*"You are what you eat."*

*"Association causes affiliation."*

*"If you hang out with dogs you will get fleas."*

This last quote is my mom's favorite that my sibling and I heard while growing up.

She would always say:

*"Pay close attention to the company that you keep,*

*And the people you surround yourself with."*

These were her daily words of wisdom throughout our childhood.

My father would always tell me:

*"After you graduate from high school you will be lucky to have two real friends in life because friendship comes at a high cost."*

**Thank you in advance.**

As we journey through this book you will see quotes from friends who have chosen to give input, and shine light on some of their own personal experiences good or bad.

## John 8:32

**"And ye shall know the truth and the truth shall make you free."**

**If anything in this book hits you in a personal way just say ouch learn from it and become better.**

**I did not write to offend put to shine light on our mistakes.**

# ℬDISCLOSURES℘

Real names will not be used; participants will be given aliases to protect their identity for the lack of observation on their parts in particular situations.

No royalties will be given for bad experiences. ☺

The editing of this book does not include eliminating Ebonics.

The point of views and quotes in this book are not representative of the editor.


Since this is a Self-Evaluation book throughout the chapters we will continue to ask questions so we can evaluate ourselves. You will see red flags, footnote and bookmarks to help you throughout the book. Be as honest as possible, this is the only way we can become better in our relationships.

# "All Wrong"

## *Mistakes we make in relationship*

## *Let's move forward into relationships:*

Now that I have gotten your attention, let us begin with some key things to look out for in relationships for men, and women.

*Chapter 1 - Choices*

*Let's examine choices*

Making the proper choice seems so easy. However, most of us fight with this daily whether it is our jobs, school, home, our children, or other events in our lives. Let us start by examining women and young ladies' bad experiences when making choices.

## Bad experiences:

We will break bad experiences into two groups.

## Group One:

### Great Listeners

Some young ladies are great listeners and you try sharing some wisdom, and your bad experiences with them. Hopefully so that they do not fall into the same traps and pitfalls as you did when you were younger. When talking to them they become annoyed, and think your being judgmental when you are trying to tell them about the different situations they have gotten themselves into.

First they tell you about what their friends said, who for the most part have no more experience or less experience than they do. The sad part is whatever their friends say to them is like **gold**. They believe every word that comes out their friend's mouth. Their loyalty to their friends is unmeasured even to the point of allowing their friends to go through hardships instead of being a **real friend**, and helping them to seek wisdom from a more experienced person.

Too many times we keep hearing friends say, "*I'm not going to judge my friend, I will just be there for her when she needs me.*" What you are really saying is, "*dumb dumb is always making a fool of herself, here we go again."* When she falls again like an idiot for not listening to what we said. I will be there to lie to her and tell her, *"It's alright girl, and what he did to you is not your fault boo boo."*

## We're going to title this:

*"Misery loves company"*

## Bookmark:

A <u>real</u> friend is someone who has your best interests at heart, <u>not</u> someone trying to pacify your different emotions.

## Quote:

*I was living a nightmare it seems, having three children being a single parent mom trying to give them the best I had to offer. My oldest daughter turned 15 and I just knew I was going to have some help with my two younger children. Little did I know she had lost her damn mind somewhere along the way.*

*I came home early one day and caught her with some boy in my house. She was wearing some of my things, heffa did not want to listen to anything I had to say anymore, lied about the incident and thought it was not that big of a deal. I told her I guess 15 is now the new 21, and I was not sure when I became the enemy. She wanted so bad to have a father figure in her life, I guess lashing out at me would be a way to go stay with her father where she thought the grass was greener on the other side, needless to say after I tore that butt up for disrespecting me, my house, her sister, and brother I told her she had to go.*

*I have come to embrace my friend's mother's sayings such as:*

*" Wherever you show out, that's where you will get worked out."*

*After the one-sided fight, that she lost, she later went to stay with her dad and quickly realized it was not Club Med with him and his extra family.*

## False Paradise:

*Paradise did not last very long over her dad's house. She quickly began saying she wanted to come back home with us. I told her she had burned her bridges over here, and will not be coming back home anytime soon. I have two other children to think about, and they do not need to see me being disrespected by their older sister. Now she feels like she is living in a nightmare with her dad and his new girlfriend.*

*"Baquita 40"*

## Bookmark:

Grass is not always greener on the other side young people; sometimes it's just burnt grass.

Let's pause and hear what **God** has to say about this.

## God's Words:

## *Deuteronomy 30*

*This scripture speaks about making choices and the consequences of your choices:*

*The words that **God** utters the most throughout this chapter are:*

*Listen & Obey*

*Blessings & Curses*

*Life or Death*

This is such a powerful chapter most people will not want to take time and read, because **God** is only giving you two options throughout the chapter.

1.  If you listen and obey, He will bless you and curse your enemies who hate you and persecute you.

2.  If you choose to not to listen, He said you will perish and live a hard life.

*My hope is you will take out time to read this chapter, and be blessed.*

*Let's proceed to group two of the ladies.*

*Group Two:*

## "I Need My Medicine"

This second group does not want to hear a word your saying. You go through long speeches and sermons. After all your examples and explanations, they do the total opposite of whatever you talked to them about previously. These choices would not be a problem that is if their decisions did not affect the very person trying to warn them about the potential dangers they are heading towards.

## Quote:

*"My daughter goes out on a regular basis, meets new guys, and exchanges numbers with guys whom she later may start dating or going out with frequently. Not really knowing anything about the guy she just met other than her attraction to him on a physical level."*

## Mistake #1

*"She never brings any of these guys around to meet the men she was brought up around in her life. For most women this is customary, but young ladies nowadays continue to go against what the norm is from the women before them. She takes for granted that she knows everything that is going on relationship wise. She really does not have a clue of what she is getting herself into, which then is followed by excuses for her misguided steps."*

*"Denisha  39"*

## Young Ladies' Excuses:

Most young ladies have stated if they do not feel the relationship is serious "why this guy should meet my family". **(Red Flag)** There are a few problems and stages ladies face when they start dating without a clue.

### Stage 1: Emotional Attraction

Emotional attraction deals with the attraction only for the man on an emotional level. (Conversations, similarities, mutual friends, and interest

### Stage 2: Physical Attraction

This deals with sleeping with a man based on his physical attributes only for the most part.

### You are now a target:

She is now a perfect **target** for certain types of guys, knowing she is naïve to the game, and she will get played.

She jumps into the relationship feet first without checking him out thoroughly.

### *"Sex can become the greatest tool to misunderstanding in these situations."*

## Let's label this group:

### *"Ms. Know It All"*

This group of young ladies is easy to spot. They are like a deer in headlights. **Ms. K.I.A.** stands out like a sore thumb, once the guy gets them talking he realizes he got one (sucker)

who will put out with very little requirements. *"Let the Games begin"* is what goes through his mind.

She says, *"My life is like an open book."*

*Thinking that's the best way to approach a relationship. (Wrong)*

## Bookmark:

Do not be an open book ladies, because everyone can read right through you and you will get played.

### Stage 3: Manipulation

This brings us to **stage 3: manipulation**, which is falling for the old *"Okie doke"* quick fast and in a hurry.

This fool could tell you the world was square and you would believe him after taking you through Stage One and Stage Two.

## Mr. No Good:

The guy attempts to keep you away from your family and most of your closest friends by saying things like, *"They're trying to hate on what we have."*

**Manipulation** is a big mistake most women face because these men who manipulate them do not want to meet the male figures she grew up around, because for the most part this type of man is **shady.**

## *Transparent Guys:*

This guy is **suspect.** He knows other men will see right through him quicker than the young lady he is dating, because her mind and thinking are clouded. So he prefers to be invisible and just avoid those meetings with men in her family totally.

## *More Excuses:*

He sometimes goes as far as to say, *"I'm not a people person."* or *"I'm more reserved, and to myself."* **(Red Flag)**

## *Footnote:*

Some guys will go as far as to threaten you or your family members to force you to pay attention and stay with them. **(Red Flag)**

## *Results of Your Poor Choices:*

The jerk in him soon comes out. Surprise! Now she wants the family who did meet the jerk to no longer have any association with him, and the ones who did not get to meet him to be on stand bye to put that foot off in his butt if he gets out of hand (edited version).

## Bookmark:

When the guy shows himself to be a jerk, which he will, you can't believe it, but everyone else including your closest friends are just shaking their heads in disbelief.

## Newsflash:

Ladies young and old:

**The guy was not about much when you met him;** any respectable person that is about something would want to meet your family. If you, as a young lady, are trying to determine how much time needs to pass before you introduce this young man to your family, you are now suspect in your upbringing. You know what you should or should not do when dealing with guys.

## Footnote:

**Stop second-guessing yourself.** In the back of your mind you know something is not right with this guy, but really do not want to hear any comments from family or friends about it.

## Footnote:

Some people are lacking common sense and book sense; for the most part will not help you deal with your relationships.

Relationships are trial, and error, listening is much less painful than experiences, so pick your partner wisely.

## Bookmark:

There are not any formulas to relationships. You have to pray that person's heart and mind is on the same page as yours.

## Quote: Mr. No Good:

*"I was with a guy who had someone which made me his #2 girl. He played me because he knew I wanted to be #1. I manipulated his time as much as I could "I thought". Later when I became #1, he found girl #2 and girl #3 and just brushed me to the side because they did the same manipulation I did when I was #2."*

*"Ariniqua 23"*

## Bookmark:

*"I guess you do reap what you sew."*

## Outcome of Her Actions:

*This fool got me running around acting like a chicken with his head cut off trying to lobby for his attention. "I guess I'm the fool now."*

*"What a waste of time and energy."*

## Guys under Suspicion:

### Pervert type guy.

Another reason a lot of guys like to stay away from other males in young ladies' lives, is most girls they are talking to are under the age of 16, and they do not want to be questioned about their own age or motives for talking to someone who is so much younger than they are. Some older guys love to prey on naïve young ladies, because their requirements and standards are much lower than woman their own age.

## Footnote:

Jailbait is still against the law young man.

You may find yourself in jail with bubba singing to a new song.

## Question:

Who's really to blame for our children's poor decisions?

## Parents Stand Up:

The finger should be pointed at some of our young people's **parents.**

Most problems today with our young people start at home with lack of home training and proper teaching from their parents.

We assumed what our parents did to us by making us earn everything when we was younger and not allowing us to do anything we wanted was something we was not going to subject our children to.(Big Mistake)

I'm trying to figure out this new group of parents who will take their underage daughter who they believe to be a virgin over to a boys house at night while the boys parent is locked up in their room assuming they want do anything because that person parents is home. **(Red Flag)**

*"A mind is a terrible thing to waste"*

I guess that's why high school teen pregnancy is at an all time high in today's society.

I call this group of parents

## *Hands off Parenting:*

Most new parents have taken a nonchalant approach to their children's upbringing allowing their children to make their own decisions with their child having a lack of knowledge, understanding, and responsibility because parents are doing way more than their children nowadays.

## **Quote:**

*"Parents are now letting their children find their own way which will be the downfall of our society today."*
*"EVH"*

*So now we have a generation we call the "Entitlement group"*

These young people feel they deserve the best of everything without any work.

*They say "I did not ask to come here" playing with the parents emotions.*

## Old School Parents:

**The beat down crew!** You all who was born in this era knows what this is. You better not let my father or mother find out you were not being respectable to an adult. This alone was grounds for a **beat down.** Nowadays parents are scared of their children and have allowed the system and government to dictate how their children should be disciplined.

## God's Words:

### *Proverbs 13:24* *

*"If you refuse to discipline your son, it proves you don't love him: for if you love him you will be prompt to punish him."*

This is the system my family has lived by all my life.

## Quote:

*Just for the record "I'm scared of my father and mother today."*

*"Author"*

## Suicidal Tendencies:

*By allowing our young people to find their own way without supervision they have become bored, depressed and suicidal.*

*Any form of rejection or being depressed, whether it is from a family member, friend or relationship; taking their life is option #1 for them.*

## Poor Choices and Bad Decisions:

## Quote:

*"I was trying to explain to my daughter, and her friends how to deal with guys that live in their neighborhood who are not trying to do anything, except be a gang banging hood dude. They told me, they did not want any square type guys like the one I have ☺ (a dough boy) type. It is sad that most young ladies today attribute status of young men by their looks, or false portrayals of being a hard-core thug, going around in a riotous manner wreaking havoc on innocent people. But the person I was dating at the time had more street credibility than any of these cowards walking around in our neighborhood. He just decided to give his life to Christ, and no longer wanted to live, look, and act like he did when he was young and naïve."*

*"TG 40"*

## Footnote:

Ladies do not judge a book by its cover, just because it does not show on the outside does not mean it was never there before on the inside.

The sad part about this generation is they have short term memory.

## God Speaks about this:

## Ecclesiastes 1:9-11

"What has been done will be done again;

There is nothing new under the sun."

Then God states in verse 11 people want even remember the people who created what they're following.

*A great example was Tookie Williams who most young gangbangers don't have any idea who he was in the gang world, but he infused a decade of gang violence and killings that continues to exist today.

Society labeled Williams the poster child for gangbanging while he was on death row assuming young people would not want to follow in his footsteps to death row.

Young people had no clue who was this guy.

*Most young people are following things they know little about or its history.

## Bookmark:

Drugs and gangs have such a heavy influence on our generation today. Society and our government, for monetary reasons only, have decided that it is ok for us to inflict ourselves with drugs and continued gang violence, because they have sold their souls for the almighty dollar.

\*Truth be told *"Crime really does pay"*\*

## Statistics show:

Housing an inmate cost tax payers 42,000.00 a year with all the medical and dental benefits'

## Contrast:

To sending a person to college financial aid will barely pay 15,000.00 a year for a student to get an education and secure a degree, and live a productive life in society.

## Governmental Flip Flop:

Society once said, *"Drugs were bad for you."* And one of the popular slogans was to *"Just say no"*. That is when state and government funded drug prevention programs were available everywhere. Budget cuts have made legislation change their minds on how harmful drugs really are to a person today in society. Drugs are now being used for treatments and cures with people having medical ailments. While I do not doubt that these things help reduce some people's pains medically for a short term, I know that it really boils down to the almighty dollar. The some people in government want to legalize drugs because it pays trillions of dollars and if they can tax it and control it why not make it legal, just like they did alcohol many years ago. (Moonshine, White lighting)

## Some Excuses:

I understand that one of the things that marijuana is supposed to help people with is glaucoma. However, while you are able to see better, your brain cells are being destroyed and cannot be reproduced. This results in memory loss.

## Conclusion:

Now you have improved your vision, but you just will not know what you are looking at.

**If you're high! You won't get this!**

## Easy Money:

### Quote:

*"My daughter who is 23 was trying to be grown and get her own place so she would not be subject to my rules, and regulations. She goes out trying to find work but looking for the easiest way to make fast money with the least amount of effort. She meets a guy, and a young lady who says they want her to take some photos, and they would pay each of them $3,200.00* **(Red Flag)***. They take the photos the guy known only by his nickname gives her a $6,400.00 check* **(Red Flag)***. She later puts the check into a joint account with my name on the account. My daughter withdraws the money against my wishes, pays the other young lady who took pictures with her and spends the rest of the money. I would have not known what was going on if I had not received a call from the bank notifying me that the check that she deposited had been stolen. When I questioned my daughter about the check she later told me that the photos were pornographic photos. She*

*later tried to call the guy and the young lady on their cell phones, but both phones were disconnected."* **Surprise!**

*"EC 38"*

## Consequences of Her Actions:

*The bank, pending investigation of this fraudulent check, has frozen all of my accounts. This little mistake she made in poor judgment is going to cost me $6,400.00.*

## Parental Denial:

*Parents need to be honest with them selves, and admit we have played a part in the problems of their children lives.*

**Been there done that:** *She has been in this type of situation before while living out of state with her dad. However, parents try to help, knowing she could not open an account on her own from her previous fraud check mishaps. They just sit back and say "I thought she would have learned her lesson." ☹ (Dumb me)*

## Lessons Never Learned:

Most young people do not learn their lesson; they just get caught doing their dirt. Their mindset is: "The next time I do some dirt; I will do everything I can not to get caught again."

Nowadays, **most people do not want to change, they will just conform.**

Jail becomes a revolving door for people who don't want to change.

## Bookmark:

Ladies young and old remember some choices you make can last a lifetime. Without proper guidance your choices are learned through listening, not from experiences.

## Footnote:

Experience is a **good teacher**, but listening is a **great teacher.**

Let's talk about the difference between listening and hearing for a moment.

## Listening & Hearing:

Hearing: is audible it **does not require** any application. This action is usually determined by emotions, and misguided ideas.

This is what most people use to determine what they should and should not do, which is a great mistake.

Example: *"Girl, you know you don't need to be talking to a married man."* She replies, *"Girl, I hear you."* (Hearing response)

She is not going on the facts that he is married. She has decided to let her eyes deceive her into believing this mess she is about to get into will produce something positive.

Listening: **requires action, <u>and</u> application.**

This action is usually determined by the facts of a particular situation not by emotions, and false ideas.

Same example: Recently, I overheard someone talking about the guy who was hitting on me. She said *"He was married."*

The next time I see that jerk I'm going to ask him, *"How is his wife?"* (Listening response vs. hearing response)

This is how action and application comes into effect.

## *Pretending:*

Stop pretending what people are saying about someone is **not true,** by doing some investigation on your own the truth will come out.

## *Watch Out for Long Separations:*

If a guy really does not want to be with his former wife, he will let her take everything he has just to have peace of mind and become unattached to this woman. Then there are men who are petty and will stay separated for a long period of time not getting a divorce until Jesus himself comes back. He says, *"It's the principle,"* or, *"I just can't let her go" "I don't want her to get my money."* Or he wants to control her situation as much as possible. There are women that this applies to as well.

## Bookmark:

If your former husband stills controls things that go on in your household, no matter what excuses you make, **you and your living situation is questionable.**

**Example:** If you have to meet someone you are dating away from your house, after your divorce, there is still some form of attachment to your former husband or wife beyond the respect level.

Someone coming to visit is not a form of disrespect.

Someone coming out of your bedroom while your children are home is not a good look if you are not married.

## Question:

Do you control what goes on at your former husband's house?

Answer: NO

You had little control of him when you was married to him he is not paying any attention to what you are talking about now (hello) that's maybe why you two got a divorce.

## Differences between listening and hearing continue:

## Question:

So why is it that most people **hear you,** but do not listen to you?

## Quote:

*"When I was 15 years old my best friend talked to me about sex in a sand box. I listened and cling to every word and detail she told me about sex. Because she was older, I followed what I thought were great instructions to the letter. However, she left out one very important part while having our talk; all her great instructions **could get me pregnant.** Needless to say after this great advice, sneaking around and experimenting with a young man, I had to explain to my family how I became pregnant meanwhile telling them I was not sexually active."*

*"Wendella 36"*

## Footnote:

Remember, *"What you do in the dark shall come to the light."*

## Repercussions of Her Actions:

*"Needless to say the outcomes of my actions lead me to becoming a young single teen parent. You know after the young man found out I was pregnant his comments included: "How do I know it's mine." "I don't need a baby in my life*

*right now." "You need to get an abortion." Pointless to add, he no longer found me attractive, and he was no longer easily accessible when it was time to be responsible."*

## Footnote:

Most women and young ladies should always protect themselves first, and stop assuming the guy wants to be with you on a family level no matter what he says out of his mouth because most guys are not very responsible.

## Making the Proper Choice:

So when choosing to lay down with someone, ladies remember; in **God's** eyes that is where your **choice** stops. **Everything after that are the consequences of your actions.** You become a willing participant in the procreation process if you choose not to **protect yourself.**

## Bookmark:

## God's Words:

## * Psalms 139 *

*"Verse 13:* *You made all the delicate, inner parts of my body and knit them together in my mother's womb.*

*Verse 14:* *Thanks for making me so wonderfully complex!*

*Verse 15: You were there while I was formed in utter seclusions!*

*Verse 16: You saw me before I was born and scheduled each day of my life before I began to breathe.*

*Everyday was recorded in your book."*

## Bookmark:

Your body is not your own. **God** keeps a record of everything you do to it.

## Quote:

*An older woman told me that "There was power in sex."* Comments like these have pushed young ladies to try to use sex as a controlling tool against men. However, since what women have between their legs does not produce gold, and there is so many other woman out there willing to do what you want do. Ultimately the power of sex is neutralized.

Blame this on the **dysfunctional sisterhood (my next book)** that woman have created amongst themselves. They tell each other stupid ideas about how to handle a man.

We will talk more about this later.

## Bookmark:

*"Ladies if sex is your tool of choice then the consequences of your actions may last a lifetime." "They usually have two legs (your children) and their favorite word out of their mouth seems to be "MAMA."*

## Footnote:

Sex being a physical attribute, it provides very little power over most real men.

### Passing on Bad Information:

People say things that they have not checked into, and are quick to repeat the information to their friends. The sad part is your friends listen, repeat it and apply the information, usually without scrutinizing it beyond the surface of the comment.

## We call this:

*"The Blind Leading the Blind Syndrome"*

## Question:

Why do we listen to people who really do not know much of anything?

**Example:** A woman telling someone about staying married, when she has been divorced five times would not be the best counselor.

## *When in Trouble Who Should You Turn to?*

When you are in trouble you usually want to direct your energy, and attention to the one who can help you, and for the most part **this will not be a friend.** Majority of our friends have circumstantial kind of love for each other. This kind of love is called "phileo" which appears in the Bible and in Hebrew meaning with conditions.

**Example:** You do for me, and I do for you. This type of love or mutual understanding best describes "phileo."

We will talk more in-depth about this throughout the book.

## *Footnote:*

Even though **God** is not with us physically he is always here in his people, in the spirit of every choice, action, and movement we make through prayer.

## *Question:*

Why do we always seem to get into trouble listening to others and not listening to God?

## Double-Minded People & Followers:

Let's go to the bible for clarification.

## God's Words:

### *James 1:8*

*This scripture speaks of the dangers of being double-minded most of us have a friend(s) or a family member who says one thing, and does another all in the same breath.*

These people have a tough time making a decision on anything. They tend to irritate you, and get under your skin with their indecisiveness, which usually leads to bad decisions.

## Quote:

*"One of my friends has this double-minded problem. Three of us have been friends since childhood, now we are young adults. She has a problem of saying things to me about our mutual friend. When confronted by our mutual friend she says nothing making me look bad as if I am the only one saying things about her. Then when I call her on it she just sits there and looks silly. But later that day she calls me with a thousand comments about the situation from earlier.*

*This just makes me shake my head on how double-minded and fake she really is. I do not understand why people can no longer be real friends.*

*I knew at some point she would do me the same way she did our friend, and I was right.*

*She later told the same friend she was talking about things she felt like I may have been doing without any facts."*

# Let's label this group:

## *"Wishy-Washy"*

## Followers of Any and Everything:

This group of people has no minds of their own. Anything that feels or looks right they will do it. Not doing any research on what the person has done or the meaning behind their actions. This group has very **low self-esteem**.

## Quote:

*A friend of mine got his name tattooed on their arm and the words "strength in **God**" written in Chinese. One day while at the gym playing basketball with another friend of ours, who happens to be Chinese, he reads our friends arm, and starts laughing and asks, "What were you trying to say?" The guy responds, "My name and Strength in **God**." Our Chinese friend starts laughing even harder, and says, "It does not say any of that." Later, we went to the tattoo parlor with my Chinese friend and finds out the tattoo guy cannot speak or read Chinese.*

*"Ty 23"*

**Stupidity seems to be at an all time high nowadays.**

## Bookmark:

Do not do things with the belief of what you think it will do for you. Do it because it just makes good sense.

Whatever you put on your body will not necessarily represent who you are. Writing it all over you is a weak reminder of what you want to strive to be or who once played an important part in your life (RIP tattoos).

## God's word:

*Leviticus 19:28 "You shall not make any cuttings in your flesh for the dead, nor print any marks upon you: I am the Lord"*

## Footnote: Don't profile yourself

How you look, what you wear, and how you mark your body helps others to profile you. You could end up serving jail time for something you did not do, because you fit the profile.

## Bad Decisions:

No one wants to ever make a bad decision because of the consequences of that particular choice they made. Let's keep it real, they do not want to hear anyone say those famous words, **"I told you so."**

## Quote:

*I was with my man when I was young. I didn't really know anything else relationship wise because I was right out of high school. I soon realized he had no clue either of what a real relationship was supposed to be like. Soon after I became pregnant, we got married, and did the family thing. He cheated on me, was* **double-minded**, *verbally abused me, kept my self-esteem low and made me believe that he was the greatest thing in the world. I wanted him when I was young and naïve ignoring the obvious facts and* **Red Flags** *only because I didn't want anyone else to have him. He always was talking about how he wanted his family and nothing he would not do for his family. But in the end, I wondered which family he was talking about. It's sad to say I have been miserable for over two decades and at my lowest point in my life,* **"I even contemplated suicide."**

*"Ladies be careful what you wish for. You just might get it."*

*"TT 41"*

## Question:

## What the differences between wishing for something, and praying for something?

### Quotes:

*"I graduated from high school, and talked to different guys while I was in school, but did not have any type of sexual experiences. I got with a guy who had been in jail during his teenage years for drugs and gangbanging. **(Red Flag)** I got attached to him too quickly without listening to advice from my family, who were much wiser than me. I focused on his looks without doing a proper investigation into his past. I quickly found out **he was double-minded**, and on medication for anger management. We lasted about 3 months. He was very jealous. **(Red Flag)** He would get angry easily and apologize in the same breath. I started missing school and sneaking in and out of his mother's house disrespecting her and me. He became a stalker. **(Red Flag)** He told me he would never let some other guy talk to me whether we were together or not, I would always be his girlfriend. He would pop up at my house all times of the day, and night it became a very scary and volatile situation. When he felt I disrespected him at times while talking on the phone, he threatened to get his home girl to beat me up. Made me wonder what happened to him while he was cellmates with **bubba**."*

*"Antiqua 20"*

### Bookmark:

These incidents do not always end pleasantly. They become abusive. You may fear for your life. He will apologize. Nevertheless, when he becomes angry, he will do it again.

## Footnote:

There is never a reason for a man to put his hands on a woman. Women do not have to accept this. These men are cowards. They need to spend time in jail and experience what it feels like to have someone put their hands on them.

## Dumb Quote:

*A student told me "When young people get into relationships they sleep with the person they meet really quickly. (Stage 2 physical attraction)So if they break up with them there is no emotional attachment to that person." (Red Flag)*

## Consequences of Their Actions:

Diseases are at an all time high. I guess this is why AIDS and Sexually Transmitted Diseases are the highest between the ages of 19-24.

## Let's label this group:

### "51/50"

## Footnote:

Anytime you sleep with someone there is an emotional and physical attachment to that person. We discussed Stage 1 & 2 earlier in the chapter.

## Quote:

*A young lady told me "A man can talk about you and do all kinds of negative things to this new generation of young woman because it really does not matter."*

*This group of young ladies is suffering from* **reverse effect syndrome.**

*This is when you could dislike everything this guy does or says to you, but it really does not matter it will make you want to draw closer to him because your emotionally attached to him, and there is a chance he might change.*

### "Ladies really"

## Quote:

*"A young man 18 was not very sexually active. He was introduced to his female cousin's friend. He started talking to her because she often visited and spent the night over their house. Eventually he sleeps with her, without protection, thinking she is as innocent as he is.* **(Red Flag)** *Later he goes to the doctor and finds out he has* **genital warts, which is the fastest spreading disease among our young people today.** *Needless to say, she no longer talks to him. She avoids his calls, knowing why he is trying to contact her." (Hoe)*

### Footnote:

Young people do not go to the doctor very often. They usually go when it is only an emergency. This is why they are unaware that they are carriers passing on diseases from person to person.

Health clinics are now reporting these people to authorities as being a danger to society.

### New Sheriff in Town:

### Now Women are thirsty.

### Cougars:

There used to be a time when it could be said that guys were old, and thirsty. (**Sugar Daddy's**)

Now the tables have turned. Ladies young and old have become thirsty. They go as far as to sleep with married men, their own friend's men, even men they know who do not want them. The older women have become **cougars** going as far as to talk to and date young men their son or daughter's age. This can be nothing but total confusion for the children, while their parent tries to revive their youth to their children, and everyone else there looking like perverts.

The mindset of an adult who falls back to this is having **adolescent withdrawal.**

## Chapter 2: Investigation - Men

In this particular chapter we are going to address a few key mistakes that woman make when trying to get beyond the first step of meeting and getting to know a man. Why did I start with the woman, and not the man? I am glad you asked that question. My belief is that a woman is **God**'s greatest contribution to mankind.

## Quote:

*The greatest preacher, in my opinion, Pastor E.V. Hill, Sr. once said, "A woman is always at their best when she is not trying to look or acts like a man."*

## God's Words:

### *Deuteronomy 22:5*

*"A woman must not wear men's clothing, and a man must not wear women's clothing."*

*This is abhorrent to your Lord, your God.*

*Two keywords we want to examine:*

*Observation:* To be under surveillance, scrutiny, study, inspection.

*Attraction:* magnetism pulls, draws, and holds on to something.

*Question:* Which one of these two words do we use the most?

## Let's pause for a moment to take a few Self-Evaluation Questions:

1. What did you observe physically when you first met the person you are with or with your significant other?

2. Name a celebrity/famous person that you like. Explain what you like about them on a physical level.

Most of the answers received from the woman surveyed ranged from he had a nice smile with pretty teeth, good hair, he was cute, a great body, big hands and feet (lol), swagger, nice, mannerisms, pick me up, clean shoes, and talked and acted like he had money.

*Footnote:*

Most people who have real money will not let anyone know that, this is how they keep their money.

## Mistake #1

Although all the things listed above were good attributes to have, none of them told you anything about the man you are interested in. The list spoke of the exterior of a person, which makes up less than 10% of what a person is really about.

## Let's go to the B.I.B.L.E.

Basic Instructions Before Leaving Earth

## God's Words:

### *1Samuel 16:7b*

*"Man looks at the outward appearance, but the **Lord** looks at the **heart**."*

## Quote:

*"Worshiping things is idolatry, worshiping **God** is an identity."*

*"Pastor Frank Wilson"*

### Question:

So why do our eyes deceive us?

### God states,

*"If you really want to know someone you have to dig deeper than his or her appearance."*

### God's Words:

### *Proverbs 16:9*

*"In his heart a man plans his course, but the **Lord** determines his steps."*

### God's Anointed One

### God's Words:

### *1 Samuel 16:7*

*"Do not look at his appearance or his height the **Lord** does not look at things man looks at."*

### God's Chosen One:

King David is our perfect example. He did not fit the physical criteria that his seven older brothers had, **but his heart belonged to God at a young age.**

## Going Further Than Looks:

Prophet Samuel knew none of Jesse's seven other sons were the ones to be anointed by **God** as the king. When Jesse was asked about having any other sons, he said his only other son was out in the field tending to the sheep. (What a great example.)

David had already experienced an incident with a lion, and what **God** can do for you when you are in danger and your heart is towards him.

## God's Words:

### *1 Samuel 17:34:37*

*"But David persisted. "When I was taking care of my father's sheep," he said "and a lion or a bear comes and grabs a lamb from the flock, I go after it with a club and take the lamb from its mouth."*

This prepared David to fight against Goliath and the Philistine Giants that he would later kill.

Although David was not perfect by any stretch of the imagination, **God** said David was a man after his own heart.

**Acts 13:22** *"I have found David son of Jesse a man after my own heart: He will do everything I want him to do."*

What a great thing when God can trust you to do everything he wants you to do.

Question: How do you think God perceives you?

**Are you willing to do everything God asks you to do?**

## *Eye Contact:*

### *Let's deal with the attraction of the eyes.*

That being said, since we as humans tend to be opposite of God, and looks are where most woman's initial **attraction** lays, let's see where **Romeo** fits into your world, and how this fortunate little mishap will affect your decision making.

## *Question:*

Where does your man's heart lay?

Why is this one of the most unanswered questions?

Do you give the relationship enough time to find out what's really important to him?

## Categories and the Rule:

## The 80/15/5 Rule:

These numbers represent where most men statistically fit as it applies to what they have to offer woman.

This survey was taken by woman who date or are married to these types of men.

## 80% of Men Are Surveyors:

According to the survey 80% of men are *Surveyors* and have these characteristics or traits:

Materialistic/confused about spirituality/not focused on details/control freaks/talkers/procrastinators/sexually challenged/no goals/low self- esteem/bad boys/manipulators/self-absorbed/surface/mentally shallow/they are dogs that do bite/video game junkies/they think the world revolves around them/possessive/live with a woman/usually cheap/have no clue/liars/**sexuality is suspect**/go through droughts/XXX movies online or video/non-emotional/mama's boys/conceited/but for the most part are very attractive to a woman's eye.

Some of these men will not find it a problem laying hands on you if they feel it necessary to keep you in line. They bring very little to the table unless it is beneficial to them. They have very limited abilities in pressure situations.

### God's Word:

### *Proverbs 24:10*

*"You're a poor specimen if you can't stand pressure under adversity."*

### We label these:

### *"D.N.D. - Do Nothing Dudes"*

### Footnote:

But the sad part is they have the prettiest women you will ever meet with the following qualities: loyal, hard working, take care of their children, and the ride or die type.

I have to pause here:

**Ladies help me to understand what is it do these types of men have that makes you want to keep him around?**

### Joke:

**Can you order what they have, and seem to do to you on eBay?** ☺

The less they do, the more the women want these types of men in their lives. Women want them around as long as they put in **time**, and act like they really care about them. This is heartbreaking to me because the person is usually a jerk with her and her friends. He will stand there and do absolutely nothing when it comes to being a real man.

Usually a job or lack of one is an issue with these types of men. But women love their dirty drawers. The sad part is woman will date, and marry this type of man. Knowing he was a bad news when they met him, but for some strange reason some woman think when he meets **them** he will turn in his bad news card when dealing with you.

I just shake my head and wonder what could a woman possibly want with a guy like this?

## Avoid Questions:

I asked one of my friends about this type of guy, who she happened to be with. She never addressed the issue, and danced past my questions. She goes so far to make you believe there is no type of relationship at all and the information you gathered about this guy is totally false. So her friend gave me insight regarding this particular question.

## Quote:

*"My friend is a very beautiful person inside and out but it seems she is a magnet for these types of idiots. I went as far as to set her up with really nice guys. But she falls for the bad boy type every time we go out. When she is with this idiot you can hardly reach her on the phone. But when she is in need of some support or help, she asks anyone else but him, because*

*he is very limited in what he will and can do for her. She seems to be satisfied with him just being there and not putting much effort into anything else in her life."*

*"Jom 44"*

## Denial Stage 2:

This is when you are past the age of being considered young and dumb; which is (Denial Stage 1) **to just being an old fool.**

### Wake up:

*"Can't teach a old dog new tricks"*

## Things ladies should not settle for:

## 1. Jobless.

Men without a job will usually cause major problems in any relationship. Do not expect much from this guy; know you have just inherited another child. You will soon become tired of his games, antics and excuses, but getting rid of him may not be as easy as getting him.

*I'm speaking about the men who really don't want to work or get a job.
You can tell the difference.

### Quotes:
*"You can't pay bills with love or looks"*

*"No finance is a nuisance"*

*"VES 83"*

## 2. Know win situation.

A woman should not just want to be with a man because you do not want to be alone. This way of thinking is a **tragedy** waiting to happen on any level of life whether you are young or old. This puts the woman in the position to be stuck with a **loser** for a very long time.

## 3. Opposites do not always attract.

**Unequally yoked,** if you are a spiritual woman you are making a big mistake getting into a relationship with a man who is not spiritual.

### God's Word:

### *Deuteronomy 22:10*

*"Do not plow with an ox and a donkey harnessed together."*

### Quote:

*While delivering this sermon and talking about this scripture, Bishop L.D. Williams stated, "One animal is a hard Worker (ox) and the other animal is stubborn (donkey)." He later compared this analogy to being unequally yoked with your mate in a relationship. He then asked,*

## Question:

**Which one are you in your relationship?**

**Are you the ox or the donkey?**

I will take it a step further and say if you decide to be with someone who is unequally yoked and one of you is the ox while the other is the donkey someone will be made into a **jackass** in the relationship.

Spirituality mixed with non-spiritual forces will always be an opposing battle in any relationship.

There is no common ground between you two.

## Question:

Can you, as a woman, change the Surveyor man?

## Answer:

No.

## Bookmark:

Men are just boys grown up. Some men still have a ways to go to make it to the grown-up part of their manhood.

## Quote:

*"Whatever they have been accustomed to doing when they were young they will continue to do the same thing at an accelerated version as an adult male very little will change without a conversion from God."*

**"The Truth 65"**

## Guilt Trip:

Most women believe in their minds that they created the monster they are in a relationship with. They play a part in the man's shortcomings, because of the things they were not taught in their own childhood.

The woman proceeds to think she can change him. (Red Flag)

## The Delusion and false transformation:

Women's famous words, *"I can change him."* Those four words have made some women run to other women for a relationship. **(Real Talk)** Women say naïve stuff like, *"I can teach an old dog a new trick."*

## Footnote:

New dogs will never be able to master an old dog.

Ladies, ladies, ladies listen to me really closely. Seven out of ten men are not chameleons (they do not adapt or conform to any situation). Ladies, you accept them the way they are and truth be told they do not have to adapt because it's not something you require.

Create some rules and standards and dissect the good men from the bad ones.

\*This will not happen overnight, so until you find the right one their maybe some cold nights.

### Quote:

*"If you don't stand for something you will fall for anything"*

## Let's label this:

*"Self Affliction/Glutton for Punishment"*

### Quote:

*"Why buy the cow when the milk is free? Hello"*

*"Used shoes are not purchased very often"*

*Pastor E.V. Hill, Sr.*

These quotes are pertaining to women doing everything before they secure a marital relationship.

***Example:*** Living with a man you are not married to.

Or should I say men living with the woman, which seems to be the thing to do nowadays for men.

## The trick:

The trick is you can do more together than apart, but the joke is if you no longer want to be with them you are stuck with a roommate.

Leaving may not be as easy as it seems physically or monetarily.

## Footnote:

Most things sound good in theory until they are performed in reality.

## Quote:

*"I moved out of my family's home into a place with my boyfriend, and our newborn baby. (Big Mistake) My family told me not to shack up with anyone, and having a roommate in some instances can be an outer body experience dealing with other people's bad habits, and personalities. I told them how we could save money, and I wanted to be with my boo day, and night so we could play house without any restrictions. Later, I started to notice I had become his built-in maid, cook, and errand girl. He became comfortable with sitting around doing absolutely nothing, above and beyond watching TV, playing video games, driving my car, buying clothes and shoes all day on the internet. I started having flashbacks of the movie "Baby Boy." "Where Jody did not have a car, going to see other girls after he dropped Yvette off at work, and leaving her gas tank on empty all the time." When I would check my*

*boyfriend on it, he would say, "Don't judge me." "The man was holding me back."*

*These types of men are full of excuses.*

## Outcome of My Bad Decision:

*"Times got really hard for my baby and me. Neither one of us no longer has jobs, so we were struggling to pay rent, bills, and other things with our unemployment checks.* **My Godfather** *told me, "Men will show their worth under pressure situations.*

*Let something happen, and watch how quickly a weak guy abandons the ship."*

### Troubles Continue:

*"That was just the beginning of my troubles. We were just having one calamity after another. My health started to fail. I found out I had kidney problems. He decides to move back with his mother out of state, leaving me and my son to fend for ourselves. Occasionally he sent diaper money, not really worried about us at all. But with him not being here for us that was a big problem for me."*

*"PB 24"*

## Bookmark:

People will show you their true colors when they start going through trials and tribulations. If you live with someone and know very little about him or her personally and financially, truths being told you really just have yourself a **roommate**. They should be treated accordingly and relegated to the **couch** they should not be able to get the goodies without you knowing what is really going on with them.

## Footnotes:

**Shacking up** will never amount to much of anything, but going in the wrong direction in a relationship.

Never Compromise your values.  It usually keeps down the drama.

## Words of Wisdom:

*"I should have paid closer attention to what my family was trying to tell me when I was younger. We, as young people, think we know it all. But we really do not know anything. Learning things the hard way has life lasting effects. Especially when having children by these deadbeat men.  He may decide to leave, but will he be in your children's lives for the rest of their lives physically, mentally and monetarily".*

## Quotes:

*"Mama's Baby, Daddy's maybe."*

## Moving Too Fast:

*"I wish I could go back and be young all over again. I would do things a lot different. I ran through my youth fighting to be an adult. Now I wish I would have taken another route, and slowed down and enjoyed being young, so I would not be so stressed out in my adulthood".*

## Newsflash:

*"Woman you do not have to settle for less."*

## Quote:

*"I am a bus driver and work around a lot of men. Sad part is most of the men I work around fall into the **Surveyors' category**. All they talk about is what they have, drive, wear, and what they can do for you and to you. They have no goals or ambitions. They are very content with their position in life. Doing very little of anything else." **(Red Flag)***

*"Quineisha 41"*

## REALITY CHECK

### Conversion of a Man:

We know that only **God** can change a man. It has to be a conversion that the man wants to make happen on his own.

You can encourage him and even pray for him, but the final decision is going to be his to want to make a change.

He must see some perks and benefits to going in a new direction or he will never change.

## Men Are Set in Their Ways:

When woman meet men, they think they can change him by getting him to go and do things they want him to do. **(False reality)**

## The winner is: (Not you)

When a man is in the first stages of the relationship, welcome to *Acting 101.*

He is very submissive and does anything you want him to do until he gets what he wants out of you.

This could be physical on a sexual level or constantly getting you for a little money and even playing mind games.

He lets you get comfortable, lowering your standards and letting your guard down.

## Feeling Good:

You then start feeling good, spilling your guts to your friends about the guy, and saying things like, *"Girl, I think he is the one."*

## When really he is the one right now!

## Let's label this:

*"Town Crier Syndrome"*

This woman goes around talking, texting, blogging and tweeting about how this man is the greatest thing since slice bread. Wedding bells are in the air. She has dreams and fantasies of a man on a horse and a chariot. She starts telling all her friends, *"Every time I see my man, I can see my future."* The problem is for the most part you are still on *"Fantasy Island"* and that show was cancelled in the 70's when most of my readers weren't even born yet.

These men will go along with you to a point, and then you are stuck with just a lot of talk and bull after he leaves you looking like a complete fool to your family and friends. In the end, he will pull you away from the things you enjoy doing the most and have you doing things he wants you to do. If you have a tight knit family, he will try to get you away from your family. He may even move you out of town, so he can keep control of the situation without outside influences. I guess he says, *"There is nothing like a good at home maid."* This guy runs around with all these other females while bragging to his friends you're at the house.

The other scenario is he will keep you from going out and doing anything with your friends as a form of **isolation**.

### Question:

Should an **extrovert** date and get involved with a **introvert?**

### Footnote:

Ladies good looks, fancy clothes, and a job do not necessarily amount to a man having much of anything besides a good conversation and charm. He could be living out of his car, or from woman to woman, or place to place.

### Quote:

*"My family is very close and was really protective about outside people being brought into the family. I tend to attract the big talkers. Big talkers who start off real well, but in the end are not about much, living in the past, and always talking about what they are going to have and what they used to do. They tend to have big dreams and ambitions. However, all talk with no work is equivalent to "a leader parading around with no followers; he is just taking a walk". They separate you from your family. On the contrary, when troubles arise he wants you to talk to your family about helping bail you two out of the problems that he has gotten you into from his bad decisions. Later, these guys show their real colors. They will leave you and your family stranded, holding the bag and all the responsibilities he has created such as car payments, rent, children and excessive unpaid bills, etc...."*

*"Shavon 29"*

## Let's call this:

### *"Emotional Drawstring Phase"*

This is when men have you attached to them emotionally. They are able to get you to do anything, or buy into whatever they are doing on a regular basis without any specifics for their actions. **(Red Flag)** Since women are emotional creatures, seven out of ten women will fall prey to this type of man. You will learn more about this in Chapter 4 when we address Acting 101more in detail.

## Attention ladies:

Get a plaque and post it at your door. It should read:
*"If you put up with their mess, they will continue to do what you allow them to do."*

The next group of men that we surveyed was "The Worker."

## 15% of Men Are Workers:

According to the survey, 15% of men are *Workers* and have some of these characteristics or traits:

Self-confidence/somewhat motivated/job driven/video games sometimes/Spiritual or non Spiritual/goal oriented in situations/decent dresser/hangs out with his boys/treats his mama well/looks nice/family has importance to them/little more controlling/some live double lives/somewhat tight with their money.

They want to be the boss, but do not like to be reminded of some obligations, of what they should have completed sometime ago. They do not like the *"honey do list"* very much. Most are married but not happy, they got married for all the wrong reasons. They may have been in love, but circumstances such as their woman having a bad childhood, lack of parents in their life, or just lack of support from family, and friends makes the man feel like he must fill that void in the woman's life. She then holds this man to a much higher standard than the one she dated or was married to before. When he does not respond the way she feels he should then she becomes angered and close-minded.

## We can label this guy:

### "Knight in Shining Armor Syndrome"

A lot of guys get caught up in this **emotional feeling** knowing the woman has nowhere else to turn. The act of being a **knight** comes with good intentions, but getting married right away was not in the **Workers** plans right at the time.

## The Worker's Attributes continued:

Physically/Sexually the Worker can get the job done. At times make you see or feel like you never have before. This is where the **Worker** separates himself from the **Surveyor**. The worker after some time is not always consistent, tends to become too comfortable with routine, and after awhile loses his edge and develops a split personality, **"Surveyor/Worker."** He is mentally going back and forth in his character and actions.

## Split personality:

### Quote:

*"I dated a guy who was really nice to me, treated me really well. I started noticing a few **Red Flags** along the way. I chose to ignore them. He invited me to some parties given by his friends; he introduced me by my name not as his girlfriend. This guy was so bold as to introduce me to friends of his current wife. I was the only one that was clueless to what was going on. Clueless because I had keys to his apartment and*

*when I was with him the phone never rang when we were together. Little did I know he and his wife had an arrangement where they lived in separate apartments? After I left him for taking me through so much drama, he texted me saying the level of love we shared was something he never experienced before and realized he made a great mistake by letting me go. I guess his wife was mad at him that week, and he could not go over to her house.*

*After this ordeal I turned very flakey and lost trust in other men and may have run a few good men off".*

*"CG 35"*

## Quote:

*"My former husband I would say was a Worker. He knew he could not come into the relationship with conversation only, because when he first met me, he knew I had a child already. He had to be spiritual, and have a job/no game playing/or wasting my time would not be an option. He must bring something to the table more than just his Johnson."*
*"Roneisha " 42"*

Woman become quickly intrigue with men's physical attributes and forget to check for **substance**. That is why the gyms are full day and night with men working out. The man knows that physical attributes is a great way to get in with women with little effort and minimum thought. Some men have gone as far as to become personal trainers to get closer to women, knowing that most women have a great concern about their body and weight, taking advantage of her low self-esteem at this point in her life.

**\*This is physical manipulation\***

**Compliments and encouragements go a long way for a woman.**

The next group of men that we surveyed was, "The Producer."

## *5% of Men Are Producers:*

According to the survey, 5% of men are *Producers* and have these characteristics or traits:

Successful/smart/has an edge/looks the part/provider/have extraordinary drive/will power/independent/swagger/hard Worker/goal oriented/spiritual/family is very important/substance/opinionated/perfectionist/satisfier/go getter/animal magnetism/smells good/sense of humor/problem solver/loyal/determined/need filler/ultra competitive/not cheap.

Very few women will meet him in their lifetime. The ones that do will usually screw up and not realize what they have until he is gone.

The **Producer** is not always the best looking, but has the most drive. The producer has no equal when comparing him to a **Worker** or a **Surveyor** he stands out like a sour thumb mentally, and physically. The hang up with the **Producer** is he really does not need you at all on a physical level, because he has that part of a relationship on lock. If he finds a mate it will definitely be for love, and he guards his heart closely because most of the time the **Producer** has been through some ups and down.

## Quotes:

*"I had a **Producer** the only problem I had with him was he was too consumed with his job and did not have much time for me in his everyday routine. So I guess he had the 15% **Worker** mentality in him, he became so job driven, and did not create a happy balance with his work and our relationship he became something I could not deal with."*

*"Netia 40"*

## Quote:

*"The **Producer** is hands-down a 10 on my scale. He makes you want to evaluate why you have been wasting your time with these amateurs on the dating scene. I had a **Producer,** and did not know what I had (dumb me) and later I married a **Worker/Surveyor.** He crosses my mind many times during the day and night. Now that I am older, I realize what I want and what I missed out on, I can only kick myself. I'm sorry ladies I just got to keep it 100 percent real."*

*"Dequida 38"*

*"I met a **Producer** from out of town, thought my game was on point. I had gone through some troubling relationships when I was young and played the pimp game ever since. I thought no man could tame me. I had them running like crazy, always trying to hook back up with me. The **Producer** came in and did the damn thing. I became emotionally caught up in the relationship. I was driving him crazy while on my emotional roller coaster. I would call him for comfort and support, and before the day was out, I would be cursing him out telling him how much I hated him for using me. Because he was so far away, I knew other women would see what I'd seen in him and I would become extremely jealous. All the stuff I bragged about not doing in other relationships, I found myself doing in this one. I probably would have lost my mind, breaking and tearing stuff up had we lived in the same town."*

*"LT 39"*

## Three Things Men Will Do To Women While In A Relationship:

1. **They will** pull on your emotional strings and may cause you to start doing things you normally would not do. This is not a crime you just have to be patient and do your homework and investigation.
2. **Consume** you mentally and physically. Once he gets in your head then into your pants, you are prone to do just about anything.
3. **They will** make you second-guess yourself on what you know to be true.

*Confession:*

*"We as women need to tell the truth. We see the signs (**Red Flag**) of the man we are interested in, all their handicaps, and to some degree we were OK with their shortcomings, deciding to just ignore them and deal with him. That is until it becomes overwhelming".*

*"Lakwaneisha 31"*

## In Conclusion:

We have tried to give clarity to the **Surveyor**, **Worker**, and **Producer**.

Woman must realize that you have to be guided by more than just looks, material things, and superficial conversations that make you all bubbly inside, and intrigue you on the outside.

**When choosing a man you first must see what is important in his heart.** If you do not sit and ask a man this question, very rarely will he volunteer this type of information?

Does his heart lay with material or spiritual things? Some men are more in love with themselves, cars, and toys than anything else in life.

Material things seem to be the norm in today's society with men both young and old. I remember growing up; you could not do anything on Sunday except go to church. Now on Sundays, I see men parked outside of liquor stores wiping and waxing their cars off or engulfed in Sunday sports events. **God** is no longer at the head of most men's lives anymore. They use petty excuses for not following the man of God such as; *"He is a thief" "I don't want any man telling me what to do" "He talks to most of the woman at church" "He want be buying stuff with my money"*

## Footnote:

Although some preachers have made church into a business not just a place of worship we as believers must continue to believe God will serve justice to those that abuse his word. These are no excuses to not attend church services.

## God's Words:

*Hebrews 10:25*

"Not forsaking the assembly of ourselves together."

King James Version

**God** has given mankind all the devices in order for them to serve him first and enjoy life to the fullest, VCR, VHS, DVD, TIVO, DVR, DirecTV, etc., just to name a few. Yet man continues to make excuses as to why they can not serve **God** on Sunday.

*T.V and radio ministries will not replace the assembling of Gods people if you are physically capable of coming to church.

## God's Words:

*Exodus 20:5*

"I am a jealous **God** don't put anything before me."

**Ladies take out time to figure out what you need versus what you want.**

## Time & patience:

This will **require** some time and patience.

This will require **some time** and patience.

This will require some time and **patience!**

Because women are emotional and nurturers, **time** and **patience** are not two things women really like to do in a relationship. If they see what they like they start loving quickly. Women like to read between the lines, and there are no lines to read between.

*Footnote:*

It is what it is: if the tree is green, ladies the tree is really green.

*We will label this:*

*"Self-Infliction"*

*False truth:*

The ability to make bad decisions based on what you want and would like to be true, not based on what you need and know is true.

You will get nothing from this but heartache and pain.

Conclusion:

Question:

Who should you put your trust in?

Psalms 25:1-22

David always talks about God's ability, protection and provision

1. God's loyalty

2. Never let you be humiliated

3. Learning Gods ways

4. Gods guidance

5. God's mercy and love

With these six things in your life failure is not an option, but if you choose to put your trust in people and material things fail will be relevant.

Proverbs 11:28

Whoever trusts in riches will fall, but the righteous will thrive like a green leaf.

Proverbs 28:26

He who trust in himself is a fool, but he who walks in wisdom is kept safe

# Chapter 3: Investigation - Women

In this particular chapter were going to address a couple key mistakes that men make when trying to get past the first step of meeting and getting to know a woman.

## God's Words:

### *Proverbs 4*

*Woman are to train their children and men are to instruct them that's ironic that* **God** *set the standard right away that men and woman have different physical and emotional responsibilities. Men are to instruct and be the reinforcement for the woman. Women are to go through all the hands-on training of their children showing them all the details of things that need to be learned, because women are by nature nurturers, and have more* compassion and patience for *the most part.*

## Let's start with a few questions:

These are the same questions we asked the women, because they apply to both men and women.

## Self-Evaluation Questions:

1. What did you observe physically when you first met the person you are with nor or with your significant other?

2. Name a celebrity/famous person that you like. Explain what you like about them on a physical level.

Most of the answers that I received from the men surveyed ranged from she had a **big butt** which was the #1 answer no matter what race the men were. She was pretty, nice eyes, big chest, pretty feet, nice lips, adventurous, a flip/scrape, had a car, house or apartment, will give you money was the #2 answer.

## Definition:

*Flip/Scrape/Ratchet:* you can do them anywhere, anytime, with no questions asked. They are usually the neighborhood "hoe." They are not above a one-night stand.

Some of these women are very pretty, just misguided.

## *Quote:*

*My cousin was a **Flip/Scrape/Ratchet**. She was a very nice looking person with a great personality and a banging body. She could hold great conversations with different guys. Before the day was out, she had called the guy, gotten all of his information and was plotting on a late night run, trying to play the late night house guest. (Hoe) When you talked to her about what she had done, she came across as if she did not have a clue of what you were talking about. She had gone* *downtown (slang), and around the world before the sun had come back up. Showing Hoe Type Qualities (H.T.Q.).*

*"TB 21"*

## Let's label this:

*"Playing dumb"*

The sad part is when speaking to a lot of young ladies; they come across like we did not do the things they are doing today. So they portray themselves as if they have never done anything. That is until you speak to their family and close friends about the troubles they have been getting into.

Here is where **Mistake #1** comes into play for the men. Although, all the things men listed are also good attributes, none of them told you anything about that woman.

## Self-Evaluation:

So why do we set ourselves up for failure with looks and conversation?

Since physical is where men's initial **attraction** lays, let's see where **Juliet** fits into your world.

### *What category does your woman fit into?*

## The 80/15/5 Rule

These numbers represent where most women statistically fit as it applies to what they have to offer men.

## 80% of Women Are Workers:

According to the survey, 80% of women are *Workers* and have these characteristics or traits:

Heart driven/emotional/good **Worker**/loyal/somewhat procrastinators/confident/ambitious/bossy/controlling/hang out with their girls sometimes/most are married/male roommates/spiritual/manipulator/have a boyfriend/split personalities/looks nice/somewhat appropriate/educated/good mothers/nurturers/somewhat gossipers/somewhat judgemental.

This is a very popular group to be in.

## Relationship Woman:

For the most part, these are women who want to be with a man in a long lasting relationship, which hopefully ends up in marriage.

## Question:

But the greatest question is, *"How much will you compromise to be in a relationship with a man?"*

Most women will **move too fast.** They tend to tell a person they just met everything they want and dream of in their life. They also tell the man all the faults of prior men they have been in bad relationships with. Comfortable with giving up all the information of the things other men did wrong during her previous relationships. **(Red Flag)**

## Let's label this:

### *"Open Book Syndrome"*

### *Woman Bookmark:*

Men do not like to work hard relationship wise. So they look, and listen for easier ways to do things with the least amount of effort and the greatest amount of potential.

Women are usually in a relationship with a guy who is **not good for them.** These men are usually unequally yoked and not spiritual as discussed previously. But women are willing to hang in there with him. Most have multiple children by these types of guys. Guys enjoy the lifestyle provided by these types of women who work and provide for them, while they sit around, for the most part play video games, and hang out with friends and side hustle for money. These guys are still living in the past. These are **small-minded** men. We will discuss them later.

### *Popular woman:*

This is the woman that most men fall in love with, want to marry, and also the ones men tend to screw over the most out of these three categories we will be discussing.

## Quotes:

*For the most part I love these kinds of women. They are on top of their jobs and their families. Very spiritual which is a good thing, because "**Lord** knows, I need someone to speak to **God** on my behalf." But they are very bossy and controlling sometimes. This can be a big turnoff.*

*The world is supposed to stop when they want you to do things and they want you to become an instant mind reader, but I love them because their loyalty is unmeasured.*

*"Mike G 30"*

## Quote:

*"I love these types of women they will put up with all your mess and still stick in there with you. I lived with the **Worker** type woman for eighteen years had three children with her, and we never got married. She did not even trip with me about marriage. I never had a real job just would go out, gamble, hustle and come home when I wanted to. There was nothing anyone could do or say to her to make her leave me if she got mad I would just buy her something expensive. She had very little requirements of me. **This is my kind of woman.**"*

*"DJones 35"*

## 15% of Women Are Surveyors:

According to the survey, 15% of women are **Surveyors** and have these characteristics or traits:

Materialistic/self-absorbed/conceited/surface/shallow/lack of appropriateness – not knowing how to dress or act/low self-esteem/followers/groupies/gamers/possessive/procrastinators/lies frequently/has a **Surveyor** as a husband, roommate or a friend/very flashy/chronic liars/sneaky/**sexuality is suspect**/confused/double-minded/caretakers of men/fighters of men/supporters of men/work/mess talkers/Hoe Type Qualities (H.T.Q.)/loud mouth/but for the most part are very attractive to the man's eye.

**This group has a bounty on their head.** Because of the low down things they seem to do all the time, this group just makes people shake their heads. They are the scum of the earth that keeps most women's life in an uproar. They will sleep with your man, husband, girlfriend and whomever else they can manipulate. This group sets men up by trying to be as attractive as possible on the outside and they have very little substance on the inside. They live for the moment and the here and now. They do not get to meet mama and the family that often, but could care less.

*Bookmark:*

This is the grimy group, but their **Surveyor membership** seems to be growing rather quickly amongst new generation women.

*Footnote:*

Ladies pay attention! **The Surveyor woman could be your best friend.**

These women are very dangerous, have very little reserve for whom they do something to. There are different levels of freaks within this surveyor group. Some of these women are taking freaky to a new level.

## Multiple Partners:

If you have been with Tom, Dick, and Harry that is not a good look dating or relationship wise. When all of the guys happen to be friends or family members, a function or gathering may become very interesting.

## On borrowed time:

This surveyor group is short-lived entertainment with long lasting repercussions. Hopefully, you do not have children by these types of women. They can be hell on earth.

## Big mistakes:

Some men marry these types of women thinking they can make a hoe into a housewife. This group of women becomes bored with routine and will soon want to go out and play somewhere else after the thrills and the adventure are gone. For the most part they are just **home wreckers.**

## 5% of Women Are Independent:

According to the survey, 5% of women are **Independent** and have these characteristics or traits:

Spiritual/successful/common sense/book smart/appropriateness/great communicator/mother/nurturer/drive/resourceful/hard worker/family/unassuming/character/need filler/considerate/concerned/problem solver/loyal/value/self worth/inner strength/charisma/charm/heart driven/emotional/educated.

## Diamond In The Rough Group:

Most men will not know they have been with this kind of women until it is too late. These women are not easy to find because they are usually attached to men who are not right for them. Some of these women are attracted and attached to the **Surveyor** type man. Guy who has caused her to suppress all these great attributes because she has been with a person, who is selfish, self-centered, controlling, and double-minded.

## Wasted Time:

Some **Producer** women do not put a lot of time into men, because some men come across as shallow or insecure, given that she is a strong woman who for the most part makes more money than the man does.

Some high profile women are having this problem when trying to find a mate.

Some women will read the Producer attributes and believe this matches who they are as a woman. Truth be told, this is a hard group to join. You cannot talk this lifestyle into existence, as most ladies believe you can. You have *"to walk the walk and talk the talk"* to be a part of this group.

## Backbiting:

Backbiting will keep you out of this group. A few more things that will keep you out of this group are: boasting, banqueting, bitterness, clamoring, despise, emulation and heady.

## God's Words:

## *Romans 1:29, 38*

*"To slander or speak evil about a person in their absence."*

You have to be above any form of drama, mess and gossip. This woman is in a class by herself and want have very many close friends, because she wants to avoid drama.

## Quote:
*My wife fits in this class. She was taught well by my mother, before I even married her. She knows what appropriateness means in everything she does, how to look and carry herself as a lady. This is something that is lost in today's society. What the other groups we've discussed find as O.K., She finds inappropriate.*
*"Edwin 44"*

We have tried to give clarity to the **Surveyor**, **Worker**, and **Producer**.

Men must realize that you have to be guided by more than just looks of a woman.

Everything that looks good is not always good.

## What women will do at some point in a relationship?

1.  Absorb your time.
    This is because women are emotional and nurturers, they want as much of a man's time as possible.

2.  Take your energy.
    When they want to be bothered with you, they expect the maximum energy out of you.

3.  Over time they will get your money.
    Once you fall in love with this woman, whom you will after the first two steps, she will get your money because by that point you love her so it want even matter.

## *Conclusion:*

We have provided you with some aspects of these three different groups. We could have gone further. However, we will let you discuss that amongst yourselves and beat up on me later for telling the truth.

# Chapter 4: Acting 101

## The Introduction:

When first meeting someone there are a few key things you should and should not do. All of these things do not pertain to everyone. It will depend on what you are looking for in a relationship.

## Women's Biggest Problems:

A woman's biggest problem is **talking too much** giving up too much vital information before they even get to know the person. When women and men first meet and they are just getting to know each other, most men do not like to think very hard or talk very much. When they first see you they're attracted to you physically. For the most part no matter how much you think your **brain overwhelmed** him; it was your **physical** attributes that attracted him.

**Problem:** Not knowing how to be coy.

Ladies if you meet a man you should never answer questions directly right away. Instead you should always turn his questions back into questions for him.

**Example:** When he asks, *"So what do you like to do?"* Your response should mimic, *"A lot of things. I like outdoors and indoors events. What do you like to do?"* This causes the guy to put some thought into what he will say and more effort into the plans he will make for the next encounter. He must become creative, trying to figure out what you really like to do.

*Tip: Ladies become a challenge for him not prey.*

## Mistake #1

This mistake comes in when you tell him everything. He is going to make sure on the next date that he does not step on your toes, paying close attention not to do what the losers did before him.

## Mistake #2 Girlfriends

## Nurturers:

Women are nurturers, and they see the good in people really fast. A woman tends to become attached much quicker to a man emotionally than a man to a woman. That is unless he is part **stalker.** She then attributes all the good things he does during the **probationary period** of the relationship as to how the relationship will be. She quickly tells her friends what all he has done to her in the short lived union. (Big Mistake)

She is giving all the details to her girlfriend as if she was making a video.

## The Dysfunctional Friend:

The friend then is partially blinded because she is most likely in or has been in a **dysfunctional relationship** where she has been screwed over, and she forgets to tell her friend to take it slow.

## *Footnote:*

Stop asking your nut bar friend to be your therapist, while she is still lying on the couch at her own appointment.
(Red Flag)

## *Proper advice:*

As we discussed in the earlier chapters when looking for help you should know whom to turn to. Those people who put their trust in God himself and know he is our only help. Many will hear this and say, "Yeah, yeah, yeah." Although when it comes to putting it into action it is not as easy as it sounds. They recite all the scriptures and things that sound Godly such as "Let go let God." But that fool they are in a relationship with is still at their house that is who really needs to be

**"*Let go of.*" And you should then be thanking God**

## *God's Words:*

### *\*Proverbs 18:24\**

**"*There are 'friends' who pretend to be friends, but there is a friend that sticks closer than a brother.*"**
**"*Living*"**

Most friends at their best are circumstantial, they do for you because you have done for them at some point in your friendship, and have created a surface superficial type bond.

## The Problem: The Friend:

You put your trust in your friend **big mistake.** Baring your soul, telling her everything this guy has done and planning on doing with you. Somewhere along the line you did not take your **medicine.** You forgot there are a **shortage of men** and an even **bigger shortage of good men.**

## Consequences of Your Stupid Remarks:

Usually two things occur as a result of you confiding in your friends.

## First: Betrayal:

Your friend, homey, ace coon boon (slang), road dog (slang), or bestie (slang) becomes intrigued with your man and may even become his best friend (Red Flag).

## Competition:

Many women are competitive, always trying to outdo the other, even to the point of getting close to your man and at the cost of **betraying your trust.** The next sound you may hear when you come to his house is your friend making some **loud** freaky noises. (Hello)

### Next: You being an Idiot:

She may think you are an idiot, showing hoe like tendencies by the way you are letting this man play you, and rushing into things with him way to quick.

### Girlfriend Hiatus:

**Competitiveness** and **Betrayal** are two reasons women have abandoned girlfriends and now have more guy friends, but you know this brings about its own set of problems in today's society. *The guy friend you have now wants to be with your man also. (Red Flag)*

### Sorry Friendship:

Your friend will become **the reporter** and start reporting all of your business to any and everyone that will listen. That is if you have not already beaten her to telling everyone. (Big Mouth)

### Bookmark:

Your **private** and **personal life** for the most part should be **kept private**. On the contrary, if you choose to make it public within your circle of friends including your best friend(s), who usually have the biggest mouths, do not feel bad when you are being crucified inside and outside of your circle, as well as talked about by people you do not even know.

## Big Problem: Lack of Trust:

You are not my friend, if I tell you something in **secret** and you feel it's your place to tell others, betraying our friendship.

## Quote:

*"Keep your friends close and your enemies closer"*

Some people are usually your **enemy** for lack of knowledge and understanding of who you are.

Some people are usually your **friend** for what knowledge and information they have of you and your knowledge of them.

Acting 101 for the most part lasts six months or less. Though I just spoke to a friend of mine who told me her encounter lasted two years, before the person really came out with how they really felt.

Each individual is different you must do your proper research and homework to get a proper assessment of that particular person.

## Chapter 5: People's Ways of Thinking:

If you really want to know how a person thinks give them a simple test. You have to have a conversation with them and listen to what they talk about on a regular basis.

## 3 Categories: A person mindset

## Small-Minded People:

These people always talk about things in the past. Their conversations consist of, *"I used to have a Cadillac, hoes, diamonds, money and houses."* This person is having "The Mack" old school withdrawals. The sad part, some people are stuck in their past life for the rest of their lives. This group is usually very lazy and full of excuses. They may have lived a lavish lifestyle at some point in their life finding it hard to go back to living a normal lifestyle. These people may try to buy your attention and affection living way above their mean.

This group has more talk than action.

## God's Words:

### *Proverbs 10:4*

"Lazy men are soon poor hard Workers get rich."

### *Proverbs 13:4*

"Lazy people want much but gain little, while the diligent prospers."

## Medium-Minded People:

Talk about other people. Their entire conversation is about other people's faults and dislikes. This group spends more time having animosity for others, a real cover for their own shortcomings. This group spends 90% of their time spreading lies about others people, who they really know very little about. This group loves to divert any attention off of them and place it on someone else.

This group is very popular among the 3 groups

A lot of friends spend most of their time hanging out with each other talking about other people when they gather together for events and outings.

## God's Words: Medium Mindset

### *Ephesians 4:31 *

*"A spiteful, anguish ill will towards someone."*

## Brilliant-Minded People:

Talk ideas and innovations daily. This group makes up less than 5% of the people in America. Their focus and time are spent trying to expand their horizons. Brilliant people have very little time to focus on foolishness, back biting and outdated ideas. They are very hard **Workers** and that is why they are successful.

## God's Words:

### *Proverbs 12:11 *

*"Work means prosperity; only a fool idles away his time."*

## Women's Biggest Challenge:

Is her ability to compromise herself for the lesser good? Women may get mad at this part, but there should be no room for compromise when it deals with your faith, your family and your future.

**Faith** controls the **eternity** of your life.

**Family** controls the **essence** of your life.

**Future** controls your **destination** of your life.

## The Importance of Appropriateness:

This has become a great issue with women in today's society. We feel the need to be **individuals**. Somewhere along the line we have lost some of the important things taught to us by **God** and our women of the past. **God** never wants you to forget where you came from, how you got where you are and the sacrifices that were made for you to get here.

**Appropriateness** has become hard to find in this new generation of women. This is because we have some older women living in the past trying to be young all over again by what they're doing to their bodies with surgery's face lifts, implants, butt lifts, what they wear and who they date.

These **Cougars** are having relationships with much younger guys.

**Young people** are growing up way to fast, doing grown up things, what they wear, dating older men and having children at a much younger age. This problem has expanded all the way down to grade school. Today there has been an excessive amount of indecencies with our young people reported by teachers and supervisors throughout the school districts. Young people are more sexually active before they reach high school.

The foods they eat have produced bigger bodies and have caused their hormones to accelerate and become out of balance for their age.

Tragedy is their brains and there thinking process has not accelerated.

**Physical attributes** only can go so far, after the lights come on you still want someone who knows what you're talking about.

Things have changed with people in society so dramatically, because most people are trying to do things there too young to be doing, and too old to accomplish anymore.

### *What Quarter of your life are you in?*

Pastor A. Louis Patterson asked a profound question, *"What quarter are you in?"*

I did not know what he meant until I realized that we are only promised 70 years by **God**.

- *So he divided up a man's life into 4 quarters and used basketball as an analogy.*

### *God's Words:*

### *\*Psalms 90:10\**

*"Seventy years are given to us."*

### *The Beginners - 1st Quarter - Age 0-17 (Entitlement group)*

This is when you are in the training stages of your life, not really knowing much of anything. Conversely, when you hit 16 you start thinking you know everything. This is the experimental group trying any and everything that the world has to offer without regards to the consequences of their actions. This group does not talk to adults about much of anything. **They rely on their friends to tell them what they think is going on in the world.** However, their friends are slow in thinking or just as naïve as they are. They play dumb and innocent daily, thinking their acting and lying skills are better than the other three groups we will discuss who lied and played dumb before them.

*The church and God is lacking in this group's life because parents have given them a choice, but this leads them to do things that are not right in Gods eyes, but right in their own minds.

### *Romans 1:18-32 God's wrath against mankind*

*This is not an impulsive outburst of anger aimed capriciously at people whom God does not like.*

*It is the settled, determined response of the righteous God against sin*

*This group is very opinionated with little facts to anything their talking about.*

### *Bookmark:*

*Nothing is new.*

*As mentioned before in chapter 1

## God's Words:

### *Ecclesiastes 1:11b*

*"History merely repeats itself."*

*"Nothing is truly new: it has all been done before. What can you point at that is new? How do you know it did not exist long ages ago? We don't remember what happened in those former times, and in the future generation, no one will remember what we have done back here."*

## Footnote:

### Going hard: not having any regards for anyone or anything

Going hard is a term young people use to describe no regard for authority, but going hard comes with deadly consequences. *The cemeteries are staying full of young people who went hard.

## Quote:

*"I had a friend who was like an urban terrorist he gained his reputation from his acts of craziness and disregard for anyone or anything.*

*He became a menace to society in and outside his neighborhood doing things that was not always right.*

*He got killed by someone who may have not been crazier than he was, but was just plain scared of him."*

*"A person that's scared of you can be very dangerous, because their thinking of you more than you're thinking about them".*

## Idolizing a dead man:

*The sad part is I hear people say they want to be just like he was, but I told them everyone that wanted to be like him is now dead.*

**"FK 45"**

## Time will reveal the truth:

When this group gets older they will look back and wonder why they were being so stupid. Hopefully they will live long enough to look back at their life.

*Young people are dying at an alarming rate and things want change until man reverence God.*

## Galatians: 6:7-8

*"Do not be deceived: God cannot be mocked. A man reaps what he sows. The one who sows to please his sinful nature will reap destruction; the one who sows to please the spirit, from the spirit will reap eternal life."*

## Young Adult Stage - 2ⁿᵈ Quarter - Age 18-35(Entitlement group 2)

This is the age group that feels like they know it all.

There is a great transition between high school and college for this group. In my opinion, this is the 2$^{nd}$ most influenced group of the four. This is a drug and sex driven group. Like the first group they will try anything that makes them feel better or forget their troubles. **This group feels like respect is taken not earned.** I think this group has two groups within this one group.

**18-24** is the first half of this group still suffering from 1$^{st}$ quarter **withdrawals.**

**25-35** is the second half of this group is a little less volatile trying to show some signs of change.

This is the quarter of a person's life when they usually do the first of most things in their life such as: cars, house, jobs, and children just to name a few.

This group can also be volatile and very suicidal.

## *Making the transition:*

What you did in the 1$^{st}$ **Quarter** you should not be doing in the 2$^{nd}$ **Quarter.** How you look, dress, act, and carry yourself should have changed. College students should not dress like they are still in grade school. They are now transitioning into corporate America and into adulthood. They have to look the part in order to compete for jobs.

Most owners of the jobs these first two groups seek fall into the age groups of 3$^{rd}$ and 4$^{th}$ **Quarter people.**

These supervisors and owners are not comfortable with all of the openness that is going on with the younger generation, such as the excessive piercings and tattoos. All these negatives that the see you are more likely not to be high on their *"to hire"* list.

If you are a **mother** in this **2nd Quarter** all the things you did in the **1st Quarter** and a portion of the **2nd Quarter** should be in the past. **Adult parents** need to watch their actions and deeds; children mirror their parents, so you have to constantly be an example and a positive image to your children.

Be careful whom you allow your children to be around. This can be detrimental to your children's lives emotionally and physically. **Molestation** is at an all time high in our society. Later in their adulthood, many admit that someone in their family or a close family friend molested them more than one time.

## Quote:

*"My mother allowed my dad to molest my brother, sister, and myself in our childhood and was in denial when we told her what he was doing to us.*
*She became angry with me when I reported and he was arrested and jailed for his indecent acts.*
*After we got older she would not talk about the incidents much, but did say "I looked past it because we needed a place to live.*
*She later becomes an expert to how I should rear my child and who they should be around.*
*Where were you on my watch?"*

*"Tylynn 29"*

*\*Your children should never be a sacrifice for your living arrangements and she should have been put in jail for being accessory to a crime.*

## Adults - 3rd Quarter – Age 36-53 (transition group)

This group has been through the storms and the rain but they made it. Halftime of life is over for this group. Most of the characteristics of this group are former. Former gang bangers, drug addicts, sinners saved by grace, husbands, wives, and students. **This is the "I've been there and done that group."** They have become grandparents and that within itself has changed their lives tremendously. This group has plenty of common sense and has been able to sustain their lives while going through their struggles. This group tends to be stubborn and set in their ways. This group owes the **1st and 2nd Quarter** groups a lot because we created these young people, who will not listen or respect the people they learned the game from.

## Statistic:

With the explosion of gang violence in the 1980's increasing 200%: Now our young people are killing each other at an alarming rate and life expectancy is less than 22 years of age for our youth.

## Using Basketball Analogy:

In a basketball game after the first and second quarter you must make the proper adjustments at halftime as well as halftime of your life.

Analysts say the best time to make adjustments and go over your strategies, is at halftime in the game of basketball.

The third quarter is the most important quarter of a game, because this is when you press to sustain your lead, or start your comeback.

We can also use this analogy for the 3rd quarter of our life.

That being said this group has the greatest responsibility to their children, grandchildren and society to make an impact before they leave this world. This group is spiritually attached to the **Lord** reflecting on the different circumstances they have been through. This group wins the bounce back group award every year; because whatever you throw at them they seem to make the proper adjustments.

If you are a part of this group you should look and act the part.

God has been good to you in spite of what we have done to him in our past.

## *Senior Adult - 4th Quarter - Age 54-70*

This group is known as the **"Cornerstone."** When you advance to this group most likely you have been at your job for 30+ years or retired. Most people are supervisors, or in upper management. Their conversations, actions and ways come with standards, order and decency for the most part. They should not try to look and act like the 1st, 2nd, or 3rd Quarter groups. This group of people usually associate themselves with conversations of being homeowners, having 401k, mutual funds, IRA's and adequate insurance.

## Another basketball analogy:

The 4th Quarter in basketball is usually when you have your best players in the game, because it is winning time. Just like the basketball analogy, this group is the best of the four groups, because their knowledge, experience, and understanding of what is at stake in life. This group is solid spiritually, going back to how things used to be and the things they used to do are not an option for them anymore.

## Overtime Group – Age 71- Until God Calls Them Home

This group is known as **"The Rock."** They are working on **God**'s goodness and his reasons for keeping them here on earth. Their purpose is to remind the rest of us that are still playing the game, how to make it through and win. This group have been in church and attached to **God** for over 50 years and they have no desire to go back. They know the key to success is to reverence **God.**

## Psalms 111:10

*"The fear of the lord is the beginning of wisdom; all who follow his precepts have good understanding.*

*To him belongs eternal praise."*

## Chapter 6: Other Problems We Face Today:

### Your Child's Other Parent (Father):

Old people used to say, *"Be careful whom you have children with."* Meaning children are just mirrors of their parents. Since there is no "how to be a good parent blueprint book" and the father was already dealing with a lot of shortcomings when you met him, you really should not have expected him to be a genuine father. Children need a father's **presence** not their **presents.**

This participation of the father is so monumental for the growth and advancement of our young children.

It has been proven that children act totally different with a strong male figure than they do with woman.

No disrespect to woman and the upbringing of children, but there is an obvious difference in the way children look and act towards their father.

Children need strong father figures in their lives to give them added discipline and stability.

### Sides show Bob:

Now if your baby's daddy is *sides show Bob* meaning he was not worth anything when you met him and you seemed to have seen something different in him than everyone else.

I don't know what to tell you except find another male figure in the village process of your children upbringing, so they can be a father figure your child would be able to look up to for advice and support.

## Footnote:

It takes very little effort to create a child. On the contrary, it takes extraordinary work and effort to rear one so your child may live and have a productive life.

## Using Children as Leverage:

This is a mistake people make when they have children together. It took two people to create a child and it will take two people and the village to help the child grow and succeed in life with the help of **God** himself.

## Supporting your child:

**Paying** to help with the growth of your child should not be a solo effort or an act of congress on the other participant's behalf. That being said, children should never be used to settle your disagreements with their other parent. Children are only reflections of their parents. They are not born to hate either parent. So remember, whatever discontents you may have with the other parent that is vocalized by you, family and friends are embedded in the child's mind. The child then forms a conclusion. Which can make it hard for the other parent to have a relationship with their child or children? Mature adults should never use their anger to vent through their children. Once the child grows up they will have a negative reaction to that other parent or maybe towards you. This is a result of the parent being seen in a negative light or used to threaten the child to get their act together when being disciplined.

## Footnote:

Any dissatisfaction between adults should be discussed between adults and not in the presence of children.

## Women and their son(s):

The last challenge I am going to mention in this book is women dealing with rearing their son(s). I know this mother and son bond runs deep and goes without measure. My mother is my best friend hands down. My father is my friend also, but he is the one who can best teach on how to be a man. This is something my mom knew she could not do. She could show me how a man should act and respond to a woman.

I want to give much respect to the single parent mothers who have had to rear their children alone without a father in their child's life. Special thanks to the women who have took on this task with their son(s); **God** will bless you for having to play both roles as a mother and a father. Taking care of and rearing a son(s) is one of the toughest things a woman can do solo. Women were not made to be the enforcer and the nurturer at the same time by God, but with the lack of participation and availability of men, women have had to play a dual role. In honor of this, may **God** bless you with a double portion of health and strength is my prayer?

## Quote:

*"I was a single parent mom having to rear 3 girls and 4 boys alone, because I refused to be treated any kind of way physically and emotionally by their father.*

*Life was not easy living in the projects while working as a housekeeper.*

*Being a single parent mom left its share of mental scars.*

*The key to making it was I tried to instill Jesus into my children heart and they will have to live with their decisions & choices they make good or bad."*

*"VS 85"*

## A Horrible Statistic:

One of the problems we face is over **3 million male Hispanics and black men are incarcerated.** This is tragic, and the numbers seems to continue to grow daily. This is because society has decided that **crime pays,** making the jail system a big business.

## Quote:

*"Jail is not **rehabilitation,** but **restitution.** When you get out the chances of you going back to jail is great, while the odds of you staying out are very slim."*

*"Fats 45"*

*"You can come out of jail fully qualified with skills, trades and a high school degree the system will just pass you by for the most part if you have a criminal record.*

*Background checks, recessions and things of that nature have made it almost impossible to secure a job as a former convict even with all the programs the states provides for working inmates back into society."*

The former inmate after being out for some time not finding any employment now has to go back to survival mode doing some of the things that landed him in jail the first or second time and these actions could cause him to get arrested and get a 3<sup>rd</sup> strike and become incarcerated for the rest of his life.

**This becomes a no win situation.**

## Men's Frustrations

### Dual Households:

The men who are not in jail become frustrated fathers. Their frustrations stems from having multiple families to deal with. Not to mention the mother trying to control the situation in the man's other household. She decides not to let the father play a part in their child's life, because she wants to dictate who their children can be around and what their dad can and cannot do. This will always create friction between the parents, which places their children right in the middle of the parents' feuding. Men by nature are not nurturers and are more physical than emotional. So the man decides to walk away when the woman chooses to play hard ball. This will only hurt the child in the long run.

### *I feel a court date coming on:*

Everyone breaks out their papers, pictures, and receipts before the judge and in the end the only people that benefit are the lawyers, and the court system for enforcement fees they will receive.

One person will be paying out a ridiculous amount and the other will only receive a portion.

## Footnote:

Parents should try to resolve their payment arrangement between each other have it notarized just in case the person forgets their obligations and then you can let the courts enforce it.

Once the court system gets involved for the most part it's all downhill.

There are now deadbeat mom's in this generation of young people.

*So we can't totally blame it all on the men.*

Reflect on what was mentioned in the earlier chapters, men's and women's responsibilities to their children.

## Footnote:

When dealing with children you have to have an enforcer and a helper; a provider and a nurturer; a leader and someone willing to guide them, through the help of God and the Holy Spirit.

## Men's Biggest Challenge:

Male species survival is at stake. Men have come to the crossroads of their lives and must make an important decision.

## *Man up:*

Stand up become responsible men, or our male offspring will **perish**. If our young men are to survive, it will take fathers to stand up and be the men they need to be for their children's sake.

## *Words of Wisdom:*

My Uncle Robert, a 30-year lieutenant with the Los Angeles Police department and one of the best youth and young adult Sunday school teachers says *"If you want to destroy a generation you must take away the male figure so there is no ability for the race to reproduce."* With that being said, these are our obligations we face as men?

1. Accept **God** first.
   Man can't be guided by his own ideas and thoughts you will be on a short bus in for a long ride.
2. **Recognize** without **God** we are just wasting our time. You cannot be a great leader if you are not willing to follow the ultimate **Leader**.
3. You must have a job. **God** says a man that does not work should not eat.
4. You must be a provider of your household and a provider of your children, whether they live with you or not.
5. You must be an example to your children in the way you look, act and conduct your life with **God** at the forefront if not you're a stumbling block for your children and their children.
6. Men should always carry themselves as men not striving to look or act like women.

## God's Words:

### *1 Corinthians 6:9-10*

*"Not manly, a man acting womanish in looks and in ways."*

7. Men must make a commitment to **God**, family, and friends in order for our youth to survive in this world.

## Footnote:

Without a father figure our youth will do whatever they feel is right, without any concerns or regards to anything dealing with the law of **God** or the law of the land.

## Giving Men Ultimatums:

Before you start giving ultimatums to a man you must first know where you stand with him. If he is a **Surveyor** type ultimatums may work. On the contrary, if he is a **Worker** or a **Producer**, who has his own things, an ultimatum may cause him to move on. Women are amazing, how they will go through torture in their past relationships with thug type guys that have not done half the things the new guy is doing. However, they have so many requirements and restrictions for the new guy. Nothing is wrong with stating your expectations of the man in the relationship. However, you must use tact, so that your statements are received appropriately.

## Running Off the Good Guys:

Women have a bad habit of running off the good guy. They think he is too nice and pick the guy that does little, if anything beyond stirring her physical emotions **(cheap thrill).** Later shacking up with him, he becomes a blocker of other men who are better suited for you, and you can't get rid of him as easily as you got him. He is a poor example of a roommate, doing very little while creating additional expenses for you and your household.

## Consequences of a Bad Idea:

A shacking up arrangement will cost you more in your time and money. (Mentioned earlier) Not to mention the responsibility of keeping the lights, gas, and water on in addition to keeping food in the house. Your maid skills will become more relevant. My mother says, "A man can get every other kind of license: car, dog, hunting or gun license that is required by law, but will not get a marriage license if he does not have to. But you are the one he says he loves the most in this world."

*I wonder is that with the lights on or off when he is selling you this line.*

## I Am Marrying My Father:

Some women have found themselves mimicking the mistakes they watched their mothers make. Having a father in their life who is not the greatest example of what a father or man should be, whether he was abusive, drank a lot or just not home being a real father, plays a big role in who she will become and whom she will marry. When the young lady becomes of age, she finds herself being with someone with the same traits as the father figure she had while growing up good or bad. Young ladies are very influenced by their dads at a young age. They subconsciously find themselves attracted to the same type of man as they become young ladies. Contrary to the new generation, older women have toughed it out, staying married to men they are unhappy with for long periods of time, either for the  sake of their children or not wanting to be alone.

## New Generation of Married Women:

This group has decided if they are not happy for any reason that being alone is better than being miserable. The divorce rate is at an all time high, because ladies in the 3$^{rd}$ Quarter Group have decided enough is enough.  They are filing for divorce at an alarming rate after being married for 15 years or more.  These women usually feel they have outgrown the men they were once so in love with when they were younger.

## Consequences: Troubled children

The major problem with this is if they have young children. This makes it really hard for the children to make the adjustment of their parents no longer living together. They have a hard time dealing with having new relationships with people that are now with their parents. The child tends to rebel and fall off emotionally.

The children try to become the parents guard dog watching and monitoring everyone their parents are with and sometime running off people that could be a great help or companion to their parents.

# Chapter 7: The Steps to Failure

I have tried my best to bring mistakes and errors we make in relationships to your attention. I could have written three more books with all of the information my family and friends supplied me. I will save that for the next books. I have tried to use **God's Words** to compare to the thinking of **man**. Hoping this will show you why we fail and fall short.

## What I am not:

I'm not a therapist, life coach, counselor, motivational speaker and all the other things people have created.

## What I am:

*Isaiah 40:3 "I am a voice of one calling in the desert."*

## Comfort:

*The Hebrew word naham. It's deeply emotional word, overflowing with feelings of pity and concern.*

## Failure:

My last few words will deal with failure and the steps we take towards failing.

1. Making the wrong choices and bad decisions **will cause failure.**
2. Not choosing to serve **God** first, by not listening or obeying **God will cause failure.**
3. Not doing our investigation and homework **will cause failure.**
   **Not understanding what real love is will cause failure.**

   *Question:*
   A friend questioned, *"Whatever happened to just love and trust?"* I told her, "There are women finding out that the men they have been with for long periods of time are married to someone else in another city, town or state. They find this out about the guy later, because they took the person at face value, not checking him out thoroughly.
4. Thinking we know it all and really have no idea of what is really going on do to lack of listening and paying close attention to other people's experiences **will cause failure.**
5. Not taking our time and being patient **in all aspects of life will cause failure.**

*Footnote:*
We must become conscience of what we say, what we do, how we act and how we live our lives if not failure will be prevalent in every situation.

*Conclusion:*
**God** does not accept us doing anything because it feels or looks good.

*Judges 21:25*

*"In those days Israel had no king; everyone did as he saw fit."*

## God's Words:

### *Isaiah 55:8*
*"For my thoughts are not as your thoughts, neither are my ways are not like your ways, says the **Lord**."*

## We must confess our faults:

## God's Words:

### 1John1:9

*"If we confess our sins then he is faithful and just to forgive us of our sins, and cleanse us from all unrighteousness." KJV*

## Humble, Pray, Seek, Turn

## God's Words:

### *2 Chronicles 7:14*
*"If my people which are called by name, shall humble themselves, and pray, and seek my face, and turn from their wicked ways; then I will hear from heaven, and will forgive their sins, and will heal the land."*

**I have tried to share some knowledge on things we do wrong in our relationship with others and how they contradict what God would have us to do when dealing with relationships**

## ACKNOWLEDGEMENTS:

I thank God for the vision to write a book. A book that is in my opinion is much needed in today's society.

Special thanks to Tyrone and Victoria Shepherd for being the greatest parent's one could ever have.

My grandmothers, grand aunts, uncles, aunts and my siblings for showing me that Jesus is the best example and role model in a person life.